AMAZING MOMENTS

MIRACLE on Ice!

The U.S. Hockey Team in the 1980 Winter Olympics

USA
USA
USA

By James Buckley Jr.
Illustrated by Chris Fowler

BEARPORT PUBLISHING
Minneapolis, Minnesota

BEAR CLAW

Credits

Cover art by Tom Rogers. Photos: 20 bottom: © Julie Sudnitskaya/Shutterstock; 21 top: © AP Photo; 21 bottom: © Paul Hanna/UPI/Newscom; 22: © Katsumi Kasahara/AP Photo; 23: © zapomicron/Shutterstock.

Bearport Publishing Company Product Development Team
President: Jen Jenson; Director of Product Development: Spencer Brinker; Managing Editor: Allison Juda; Associate Editor: Naomi Reich; Senior Designer: Colin O'Dea; Associate Designer: Elena Klinkner; Associate Designer: Kayla Eggert; Product Development Specialist: Anita Stasson

Produced by Shoreline Publishing Group LLC
Santa Barbara, California
Designer: Patty Kelley
Editorial Director: James Buckley Jr.

DISCLAIMER: This graphic story is a dramatization based on true events. It is intended to give the reader a sense of the narrative rather than a presentation of actual details as they occurred.

Library of Congress Cataloging-in-Publication Data

Names: Buckley, James, Jr., 1963- author. | Fowler, Chris illustrator.
Title: Miracle on ice! : the U.S. hockey team in the 1980 winter Olympics / by James Buckley Jr. ; illustrated by Chris Fowler.
Description: Minneapolis, MN : Bearport Publishing Company, [2024] | Series: Amazing moments in sports | Includes bibliographical references and index.
Identifiers: LCCN 2023005592 (print) | LCCN 2023005593 (ebook) | ISBN 9798885099882 (library binding) | ISBN 9798888221709 (paperback) | ISBN 9798888223031 (ebook)
Subjects: LCSH: Hockey--United States--History--20th century--Juvenile literature. | Olympic Winter Games (13th : 1980 : Lake Placid, N.Y.)--Juvenile literature. | Hockey teams--United States--Juvenile literature.
Classification: LCC GV848.4.U6 B84 2024 (print) | LCC GV848.4.U6 (ebook) | DDC 796.962/630974753--dc23/eng/20230227
LC record available at https://lccn.loc.gov/2023005592
LC ebook record available at https://lccn.loc.gov/2023005593

For more information, write to Bearport Publishing, 5357 Penn Avenue South, Minneapolis, MN 55419.

CONTENTS

Chapter 1

COLD WAR... ON ICE

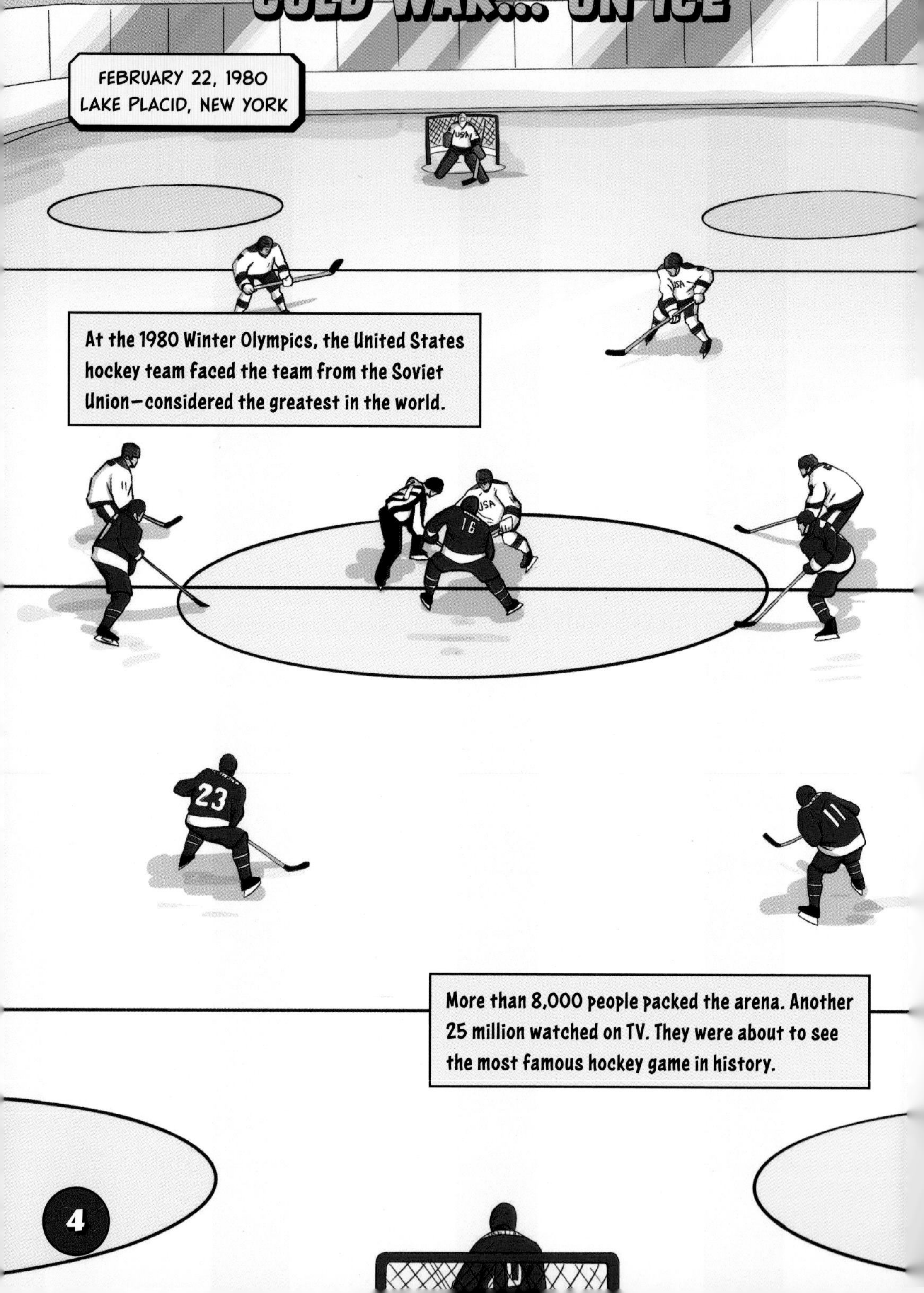
FEBRUARY 22, 1980
LAKE PLACID, NEW YORK
At the 1980 Winter Olympics, the United States hockey team faced the team from the Soviet Union—considered the greatest in the world.
USA
16
23
11
More than 8,000 people packed the arena. Another 25 million watched on TV. They were about to see the most famous hockey game in history.

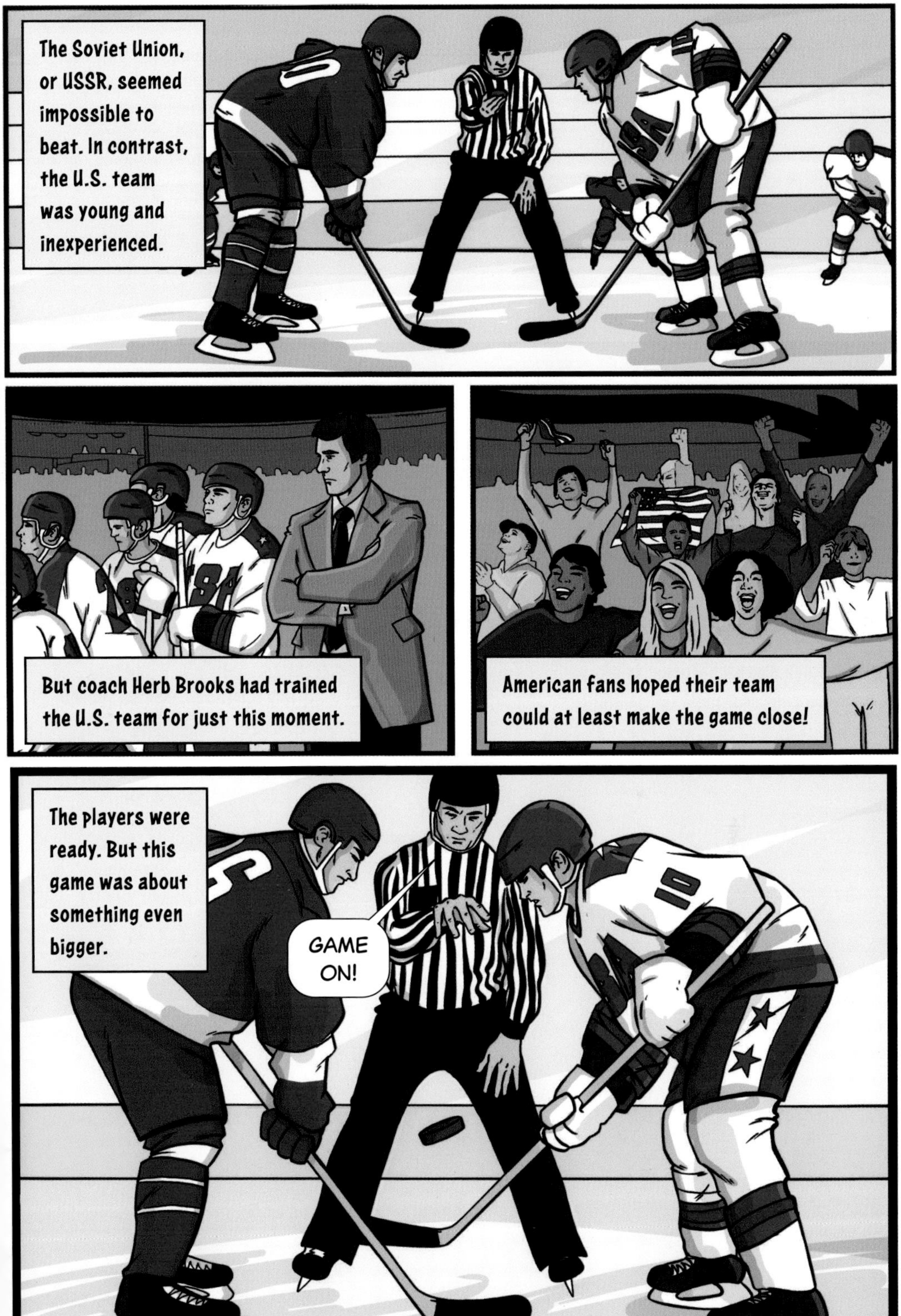
The Soviet Union, or USSR, seemed impossible to beat. In contrast, the U.S. team was young and inexperienced.
But coach Herb Brooks had trained the U.S. team for just this moment.
American fans hoped their team could at least make the game close!
The players were ready. But this game was about something even bigger.
GAME ON!

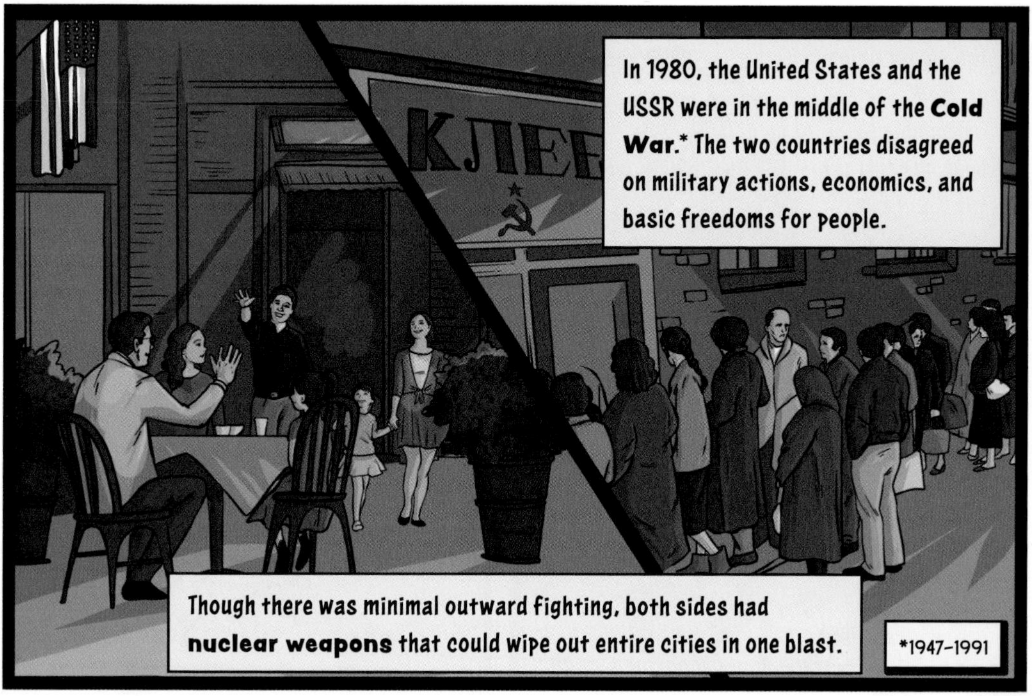
In 1980, the United States and the USSR were in the middle of the **Cold War.*** The two countries disagreed on military actions, economics, and basic freedoms for people.
Though there was minimal outward fighting, both sides had **nuclear weapons** that could wipe out entire cities in one blast.
*1947–1991

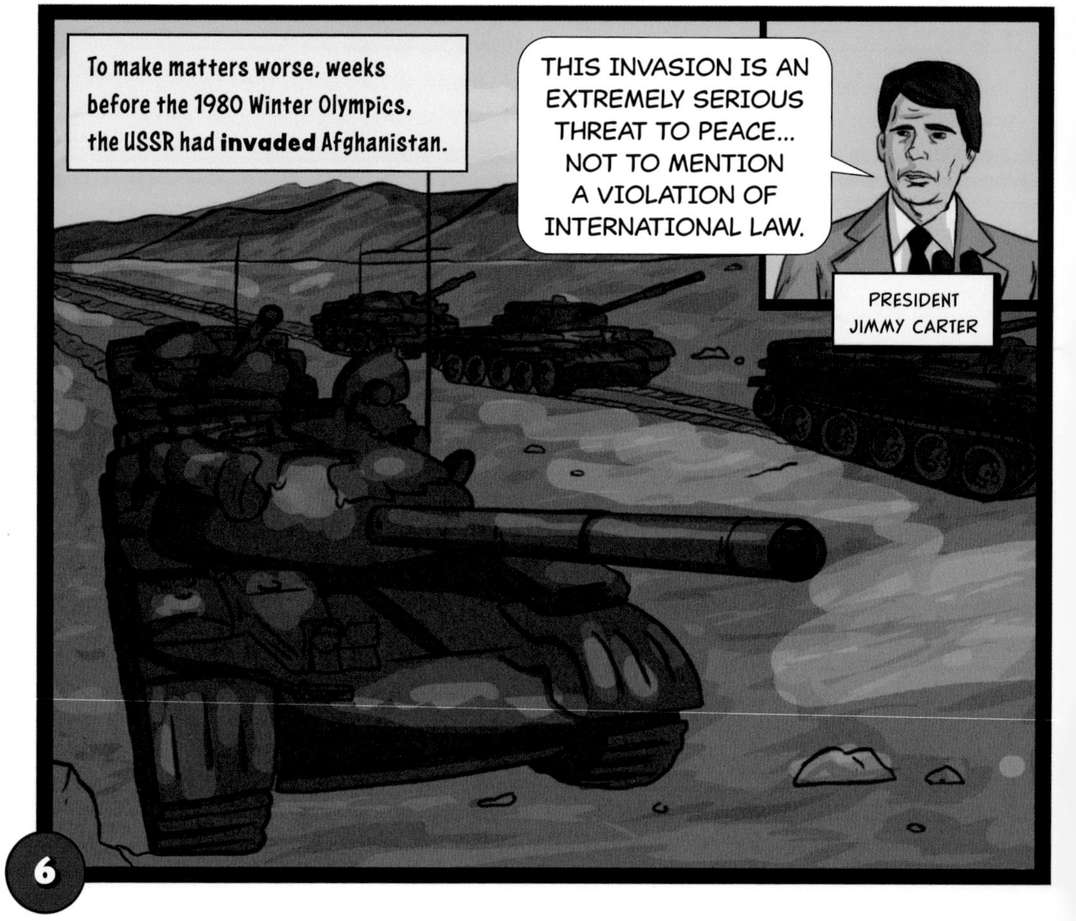
To make matters worse, weeks before the 1980 Winter Olympics, the USSR had **invaded** Afghanistan.
THIS INVASION IS AN EXTREMELY SERIOUS THREAT TO PEACE... NOT TO MENTION A VIOLATION OF INTERNATIONAL LAW.
PRESIDENT JIMMY CARTER

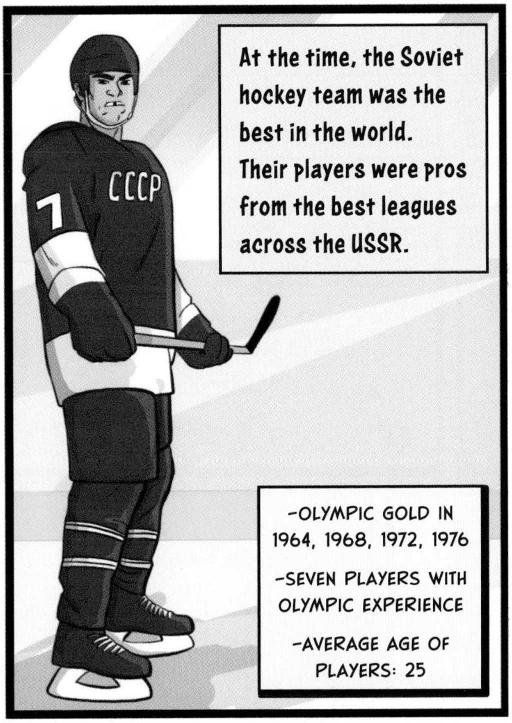
At the time, the Soviet hockey team was the best in the world. Their players were pros from the best leagues across the USSR.
CCCP
7
-OLYMPIC GOLD IN 1964, 1968, 1972, 1976
-SEVEN PLAYERS WITH OLYMPIC EXPERIENCE
-AVERAGE AGE OF PLAYERS: 25

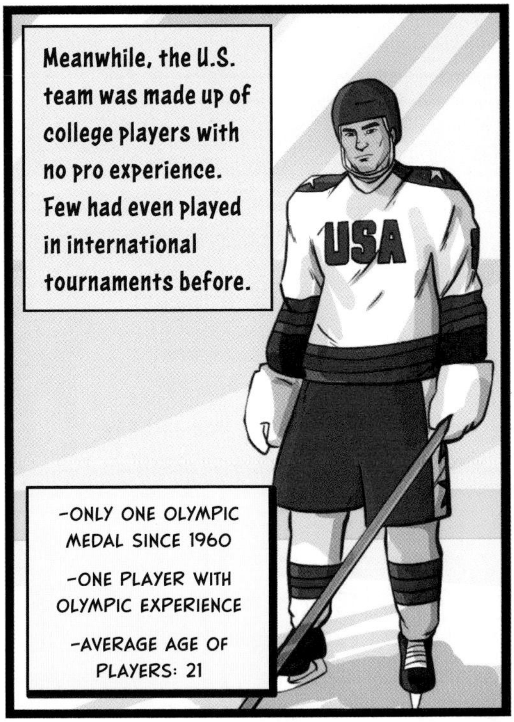
Meanwhile, the U.S. team was made up of college players with no pro experience. Few had even played in international tournaments before.
USA
-ONLY ONE OLYMPIC MEDAL SINCE 1960
-ONE PLAYER WITH OLYMPIC EXPERIENCE
-AVERAGE AGE OF PLAYERS: 21

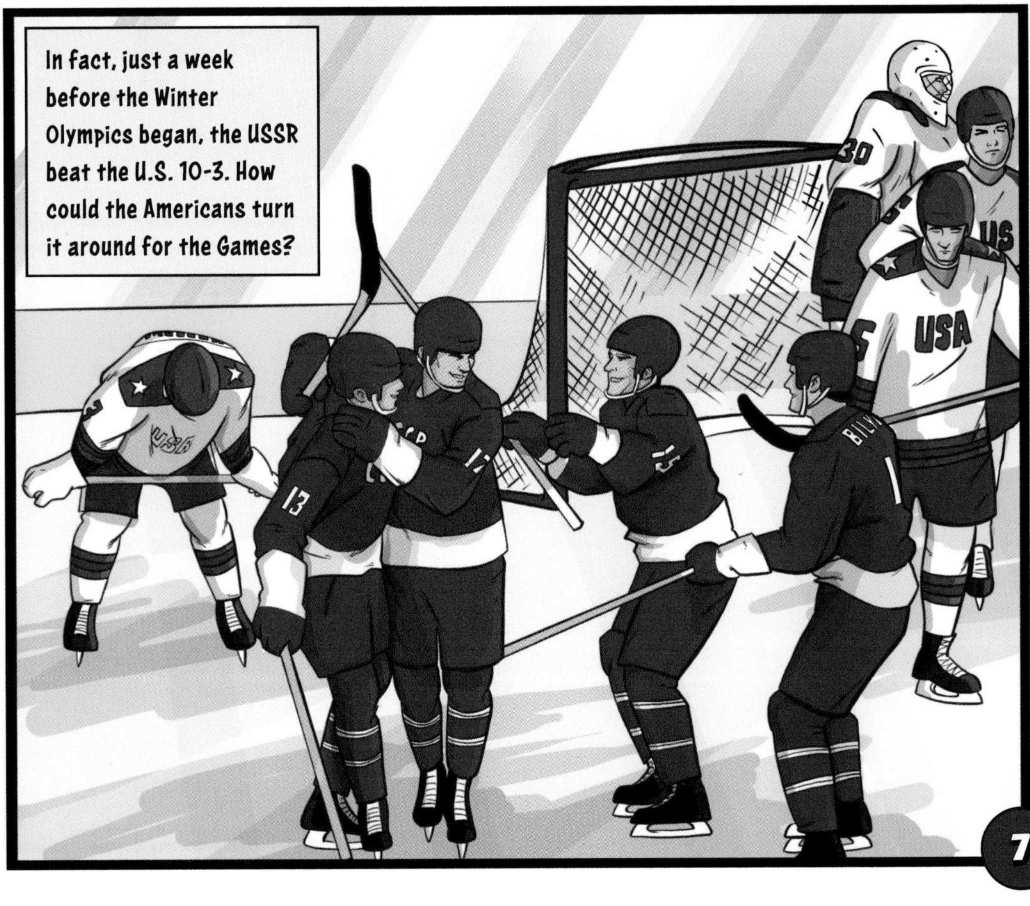
In fact, just a week before the Winter Olympics began, the USSR beat the U.S. 10-3. How could the Americans turn it around for the Games?
USA
13

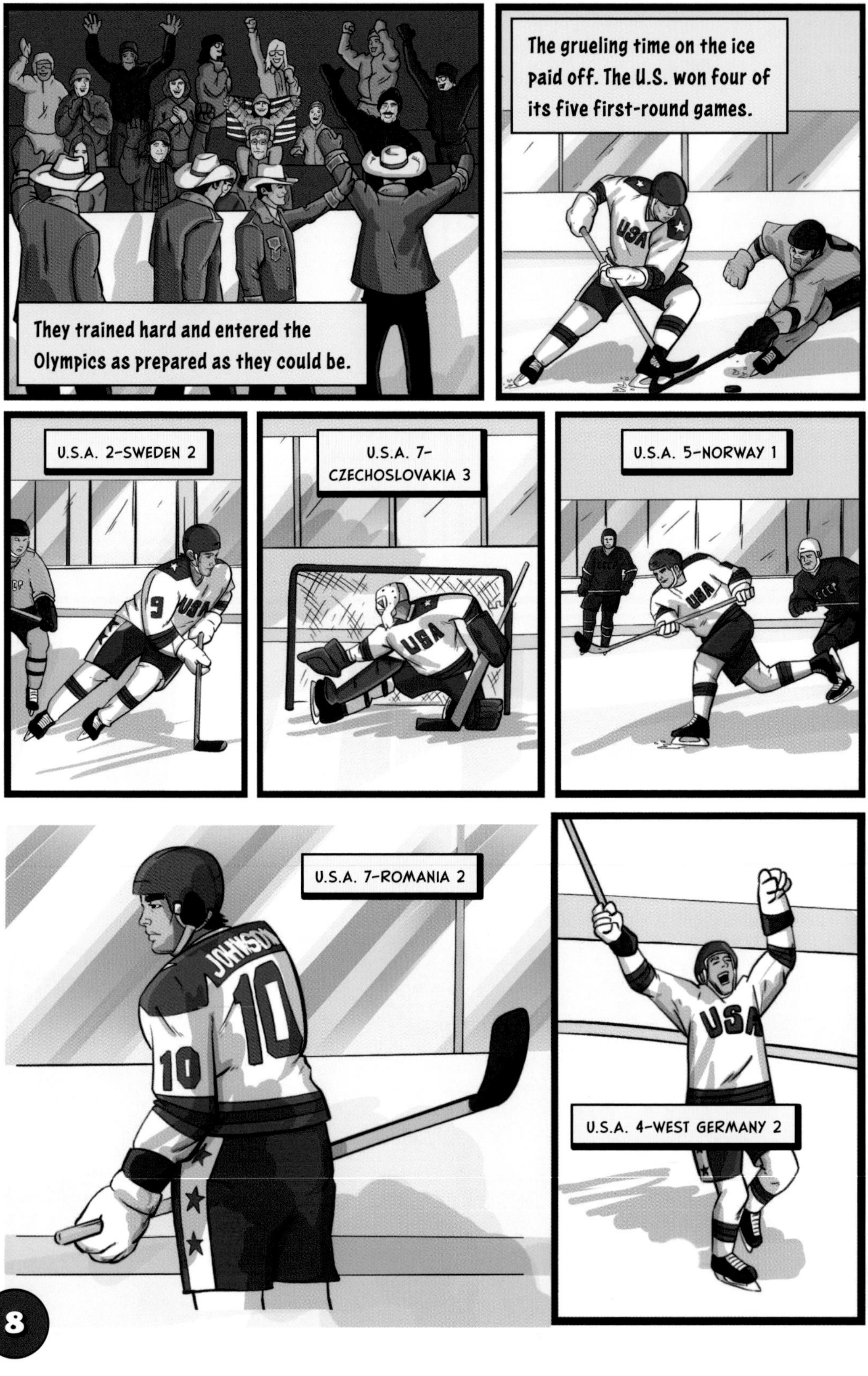
They trained hard and entered the Olympics as prepared as they could be.
The grueling time on the ice paid off. The U.S. won four of its five first-round games.
U.S.A. 2-SWEDEN 2
U.S.A. 7-CZECHOSLOVAKIA 3
U.S.A. 5-NORWAY 1
U.S.A. 7-ROMANIA 2
U.S.A. 4-WEST GERMANY 2

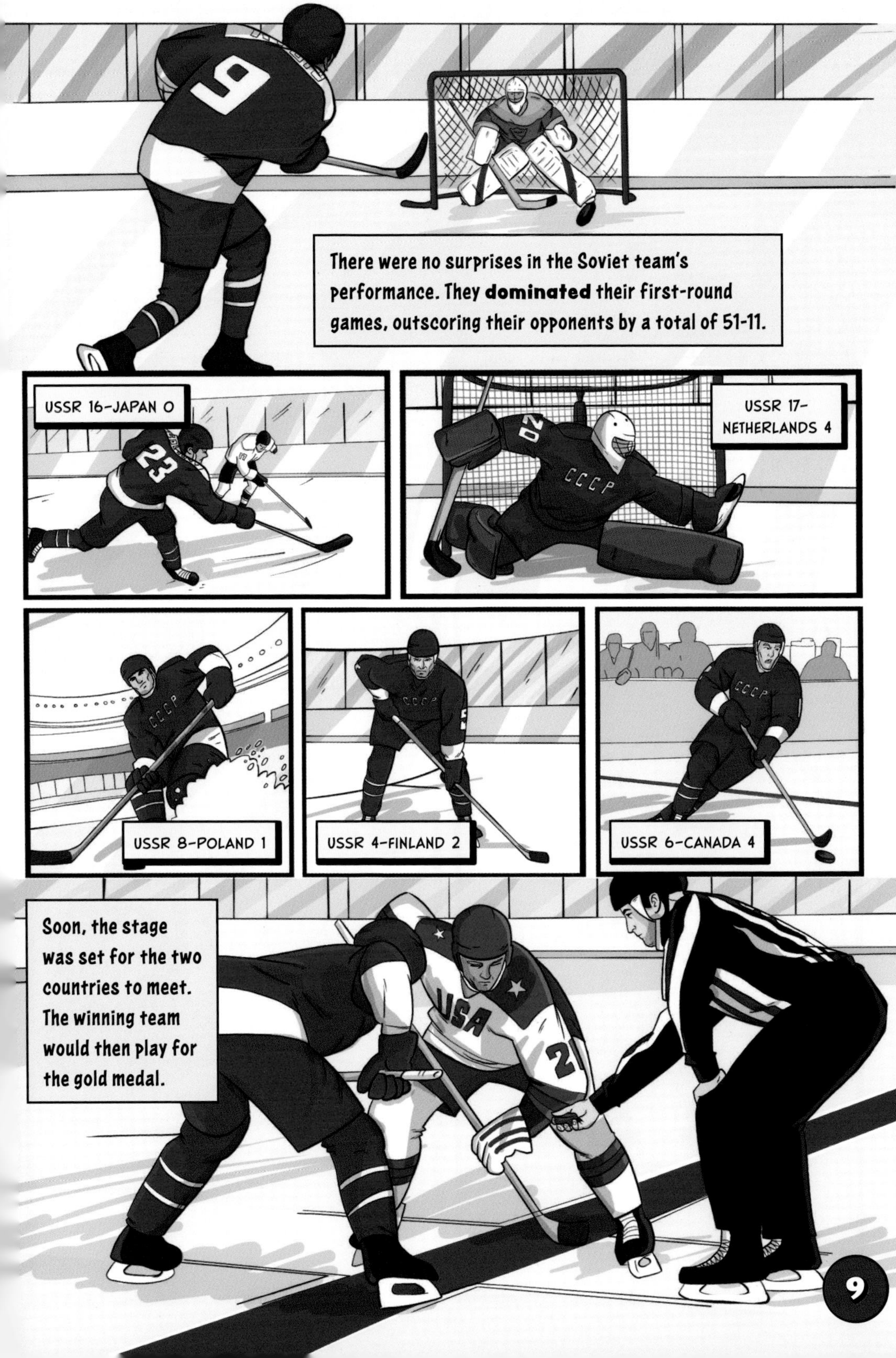
There were no surprises in the Soviet team's performance. They **dominated** their first-round games, outscoring their opponents by a total of 51-11.
USSR 16-JAPAN 0
USSR 17-NETHERLANDS 4
USSR 8-POLAND 1
USSR 4-FINLAND 2
USSR 6-CANADA 4
Soon, the stage was set for the two countries to meet. The winning team would then play for the gold medal.

Chapter 2

BACK-AND-FORTH BATTLE

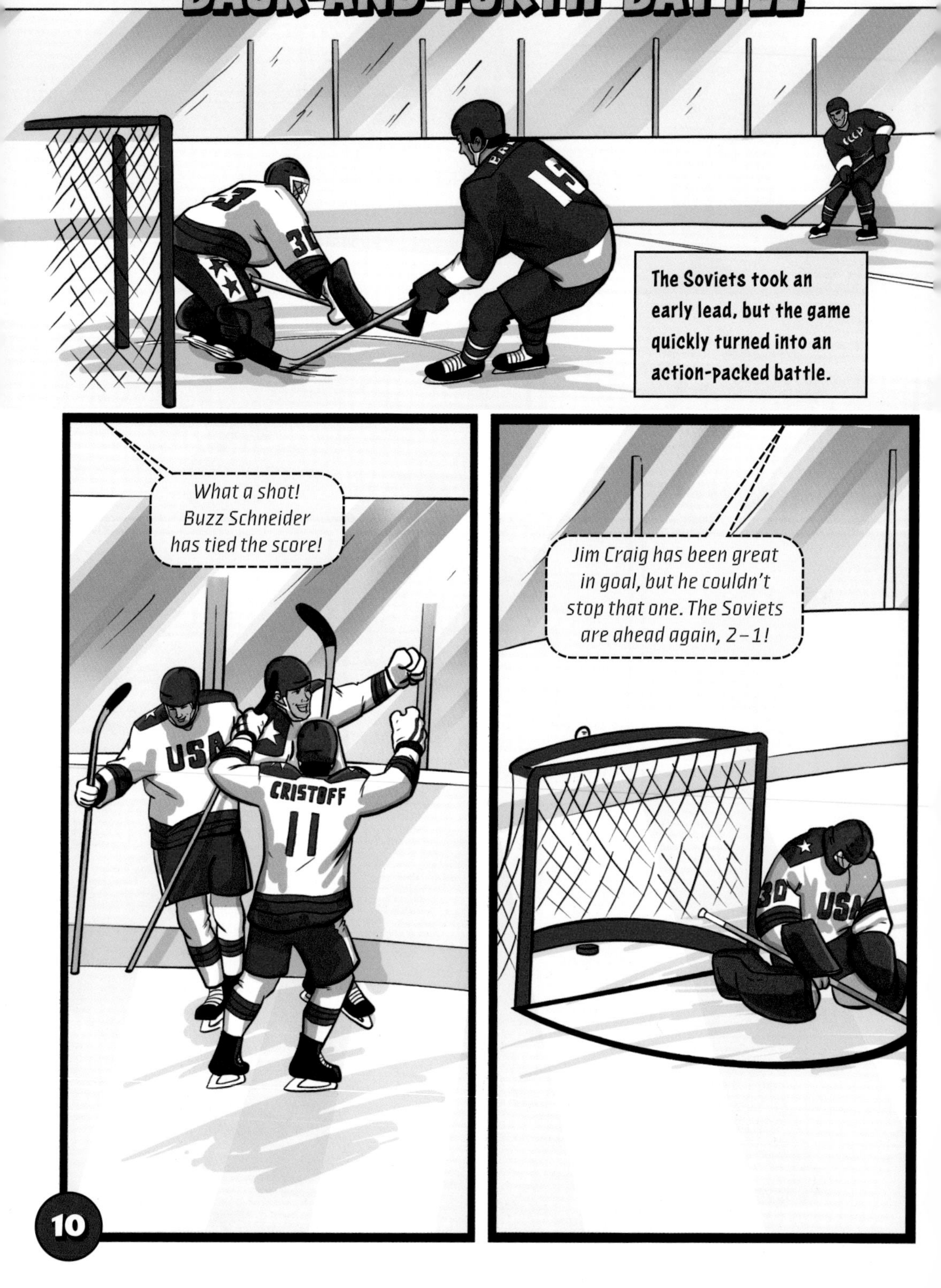

The Soviets took an early lead, but the game quickly turned into an action-packed battle.
What a shot! Buzz Schneider has tied the score!
Jim Craig has been great in goal, but he couldn't stop that one. The Soviets are ahead again, 2–1!

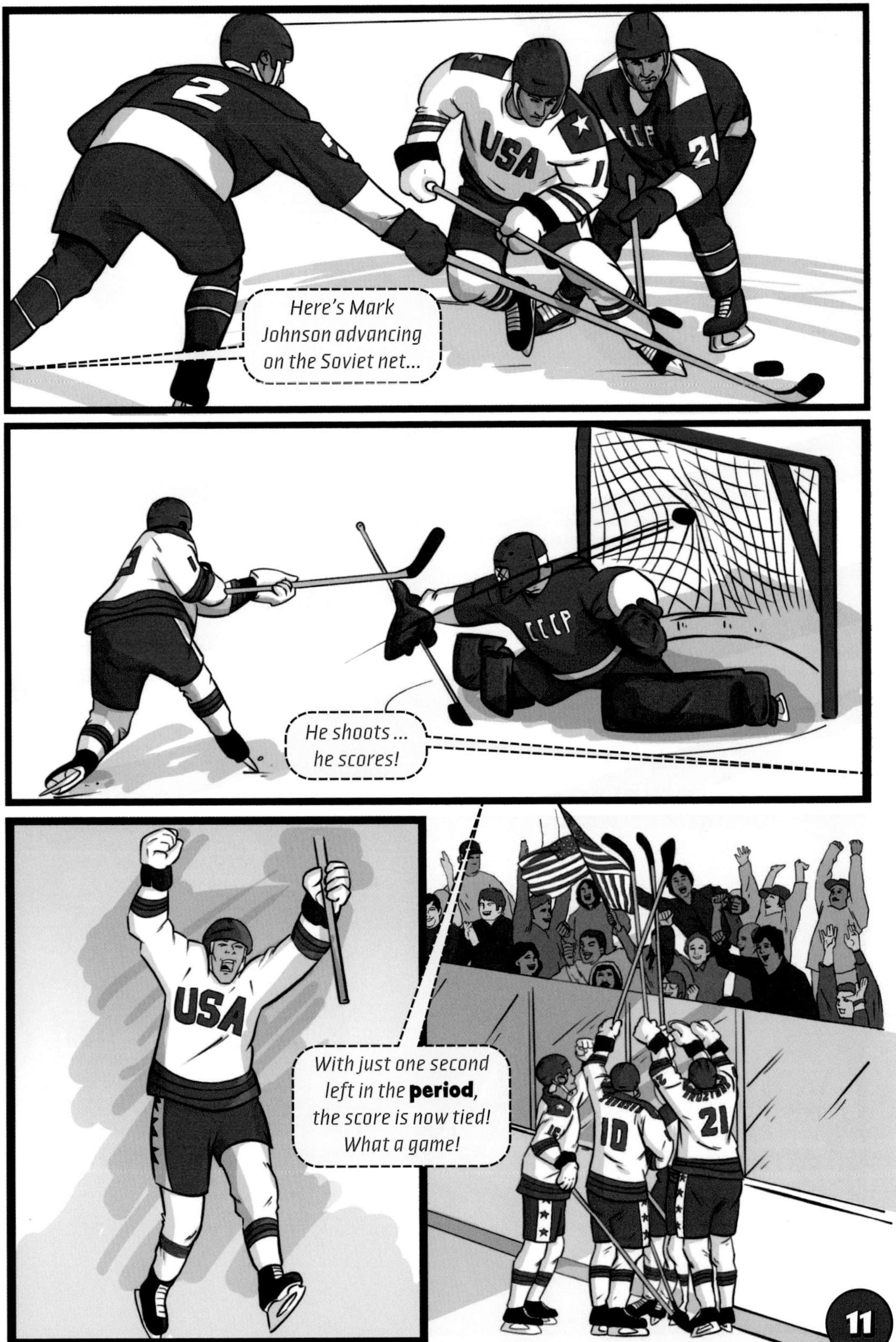
Here's Mark Johnson advancing on the Soviet net...
He shoots ... he scores!
With just one second left in the **period**, the score is now tied! What a game!

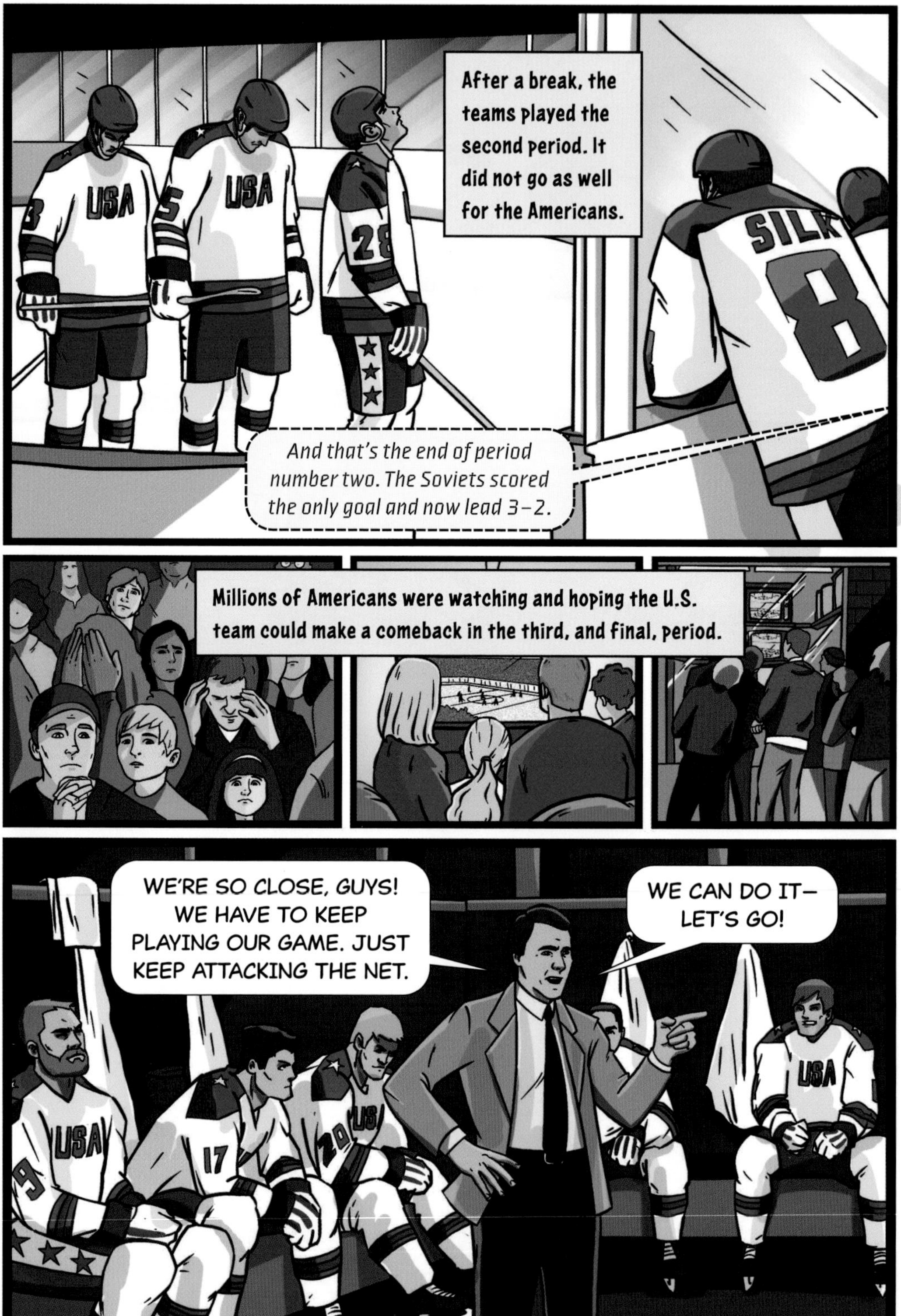
After a break, the teams played the second period. It did not go as well for the Americans.
USA
USA
28
SILK
8
And that's the end of period number two. The Soviets scored the only goal and now lead 3–2.
Millions of Americans were watching and hoping the U.S. team could make a comeback in the third, and final, period.
WE'RE SO CLOSE, GUYS! WE HAVE TO KEEP PLAYING OUR GAME. JUST KEEP ATTACKING THE NET.
WE CAN DO IT— LET'S GO!
USA
17
USA

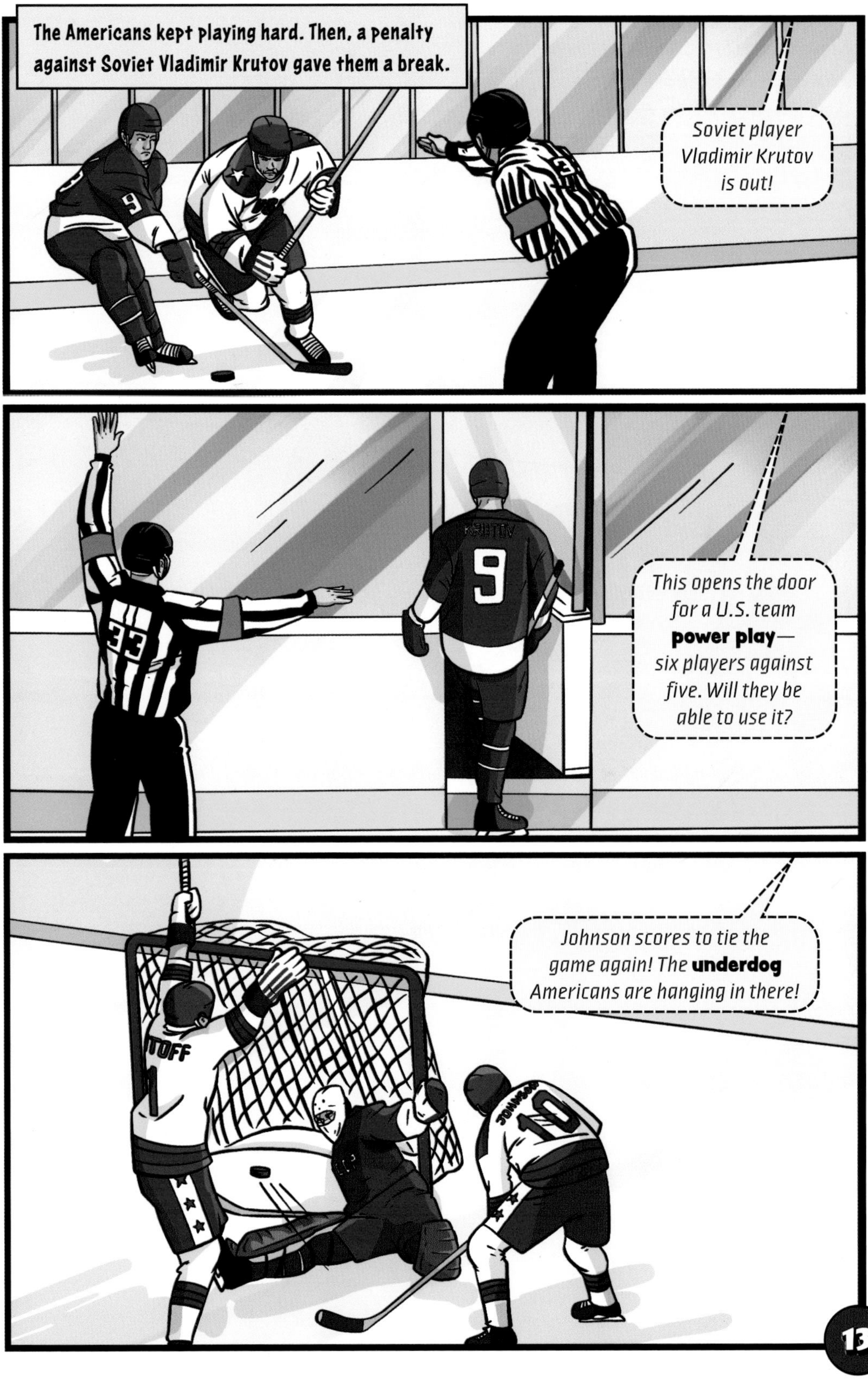
The Americans kept playing hard. Then, a penalty against Soviet Vladimir Krutov gave them a break.
Soviet player Vladimir Krutov is out!
This opens the door for a U.S. team **power play**—six players against five. Will they be able to use it?
Johnson scores to tie the game again! The **underdog** Americans are hanging in there!

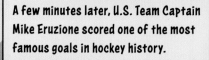

A few minutes later, U.S. Team Captain Mike Eruzione scored one of the most famous goals in hockey history.

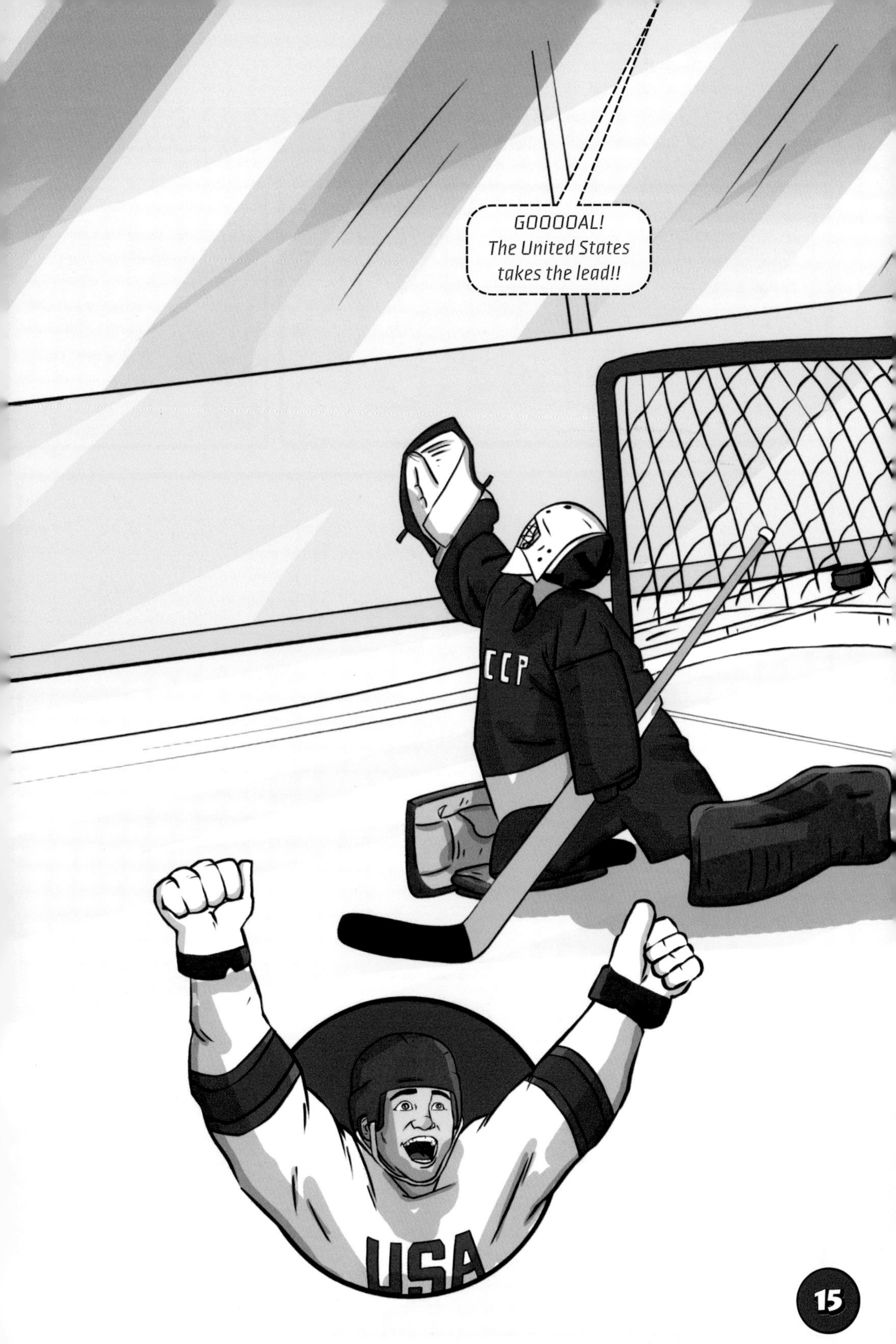
GOOOOAL!
The United States
takes the lead!!
CCP
USA

Chapter 3

DO YOU BELIEVE IN MIRACLES?

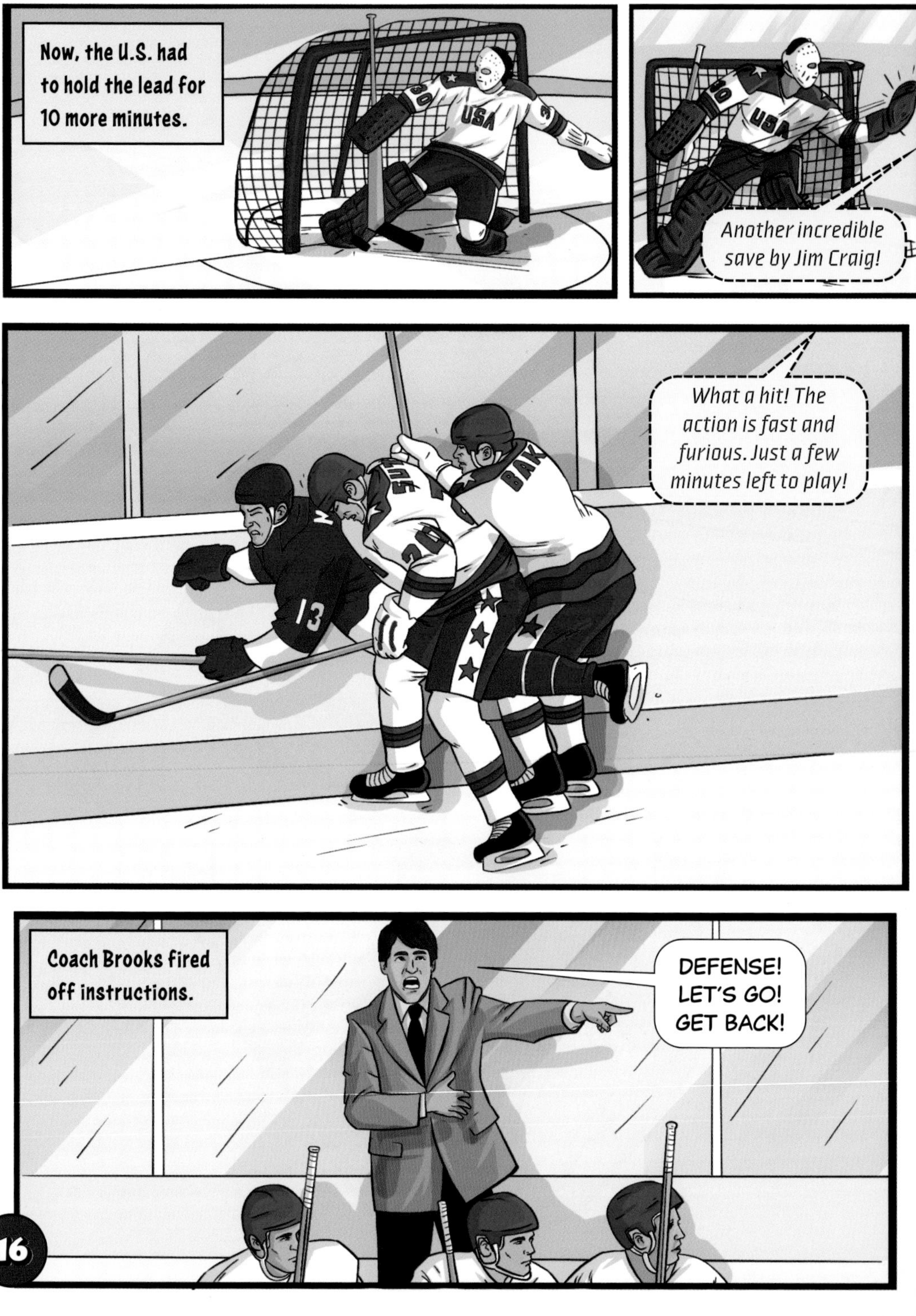
Now, the U.S. had to hold the lead for 10 more minutes.
Another incredible save by Jim Craig!
What a hit! The action is fast and furious. Just a few minutes left to play!
Coach Brooks fired off instructions.
DEFENSE! LET'S GO! GET BACK!

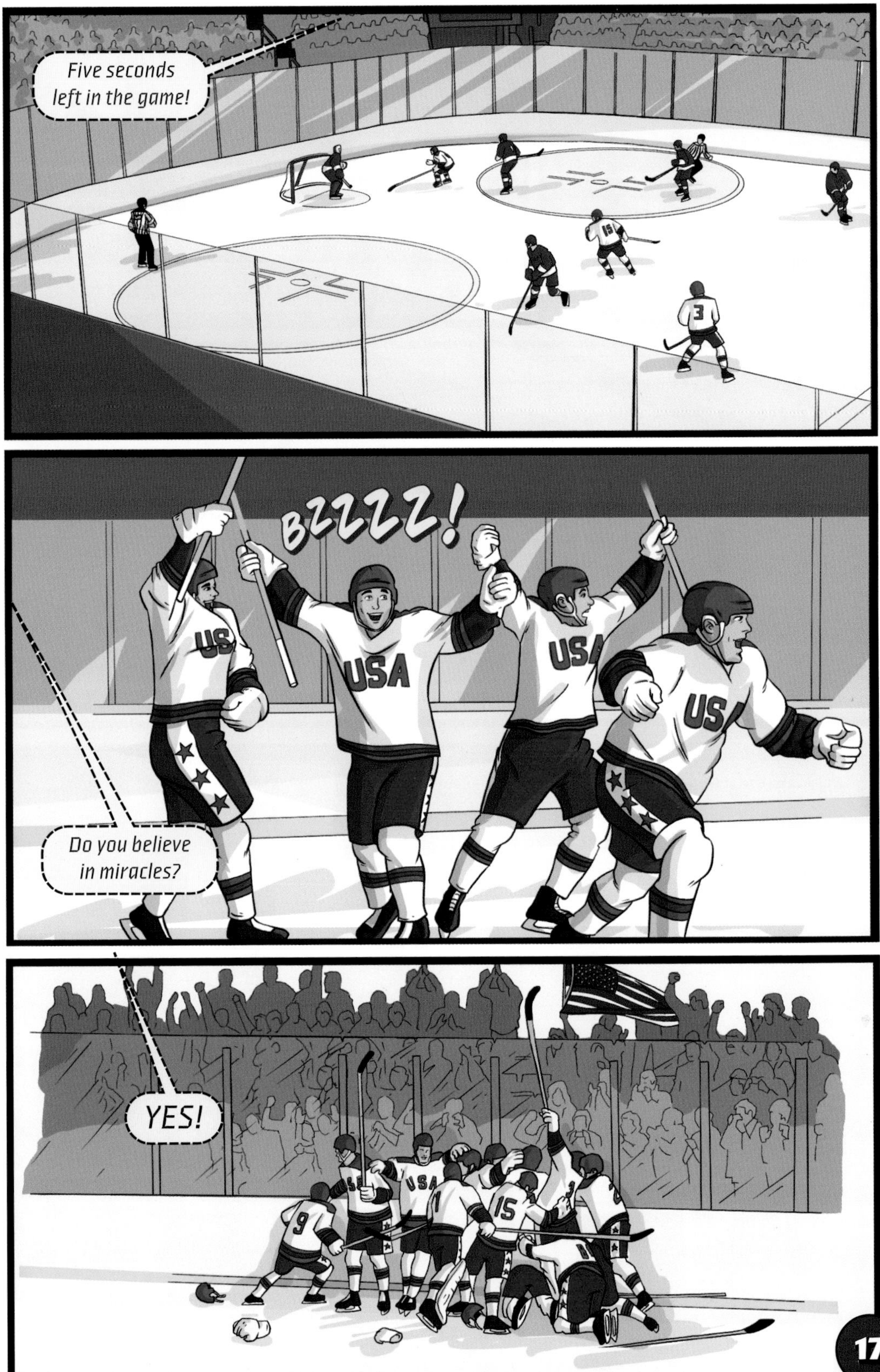
Five seconds left in the game!
BZZZZ!
Do you believe in miracles?
YES!

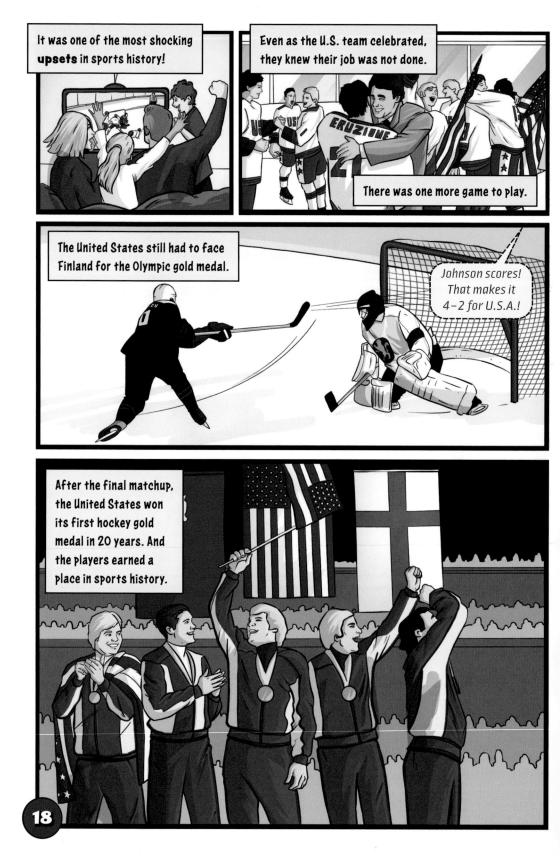

It was one of the most shocking **upsets** in sports history!

Even as the U.S. team celebrated, they knew their job was not done.

There was one more game to play.

The United States still had to face Finland for the Olympic gold medal.

Johnson scores! That makes it 4–2 for U.S.A.!

After the final matchup, the United States won its first hockey gold medal in 20 years. And the players earned a place in sports history.

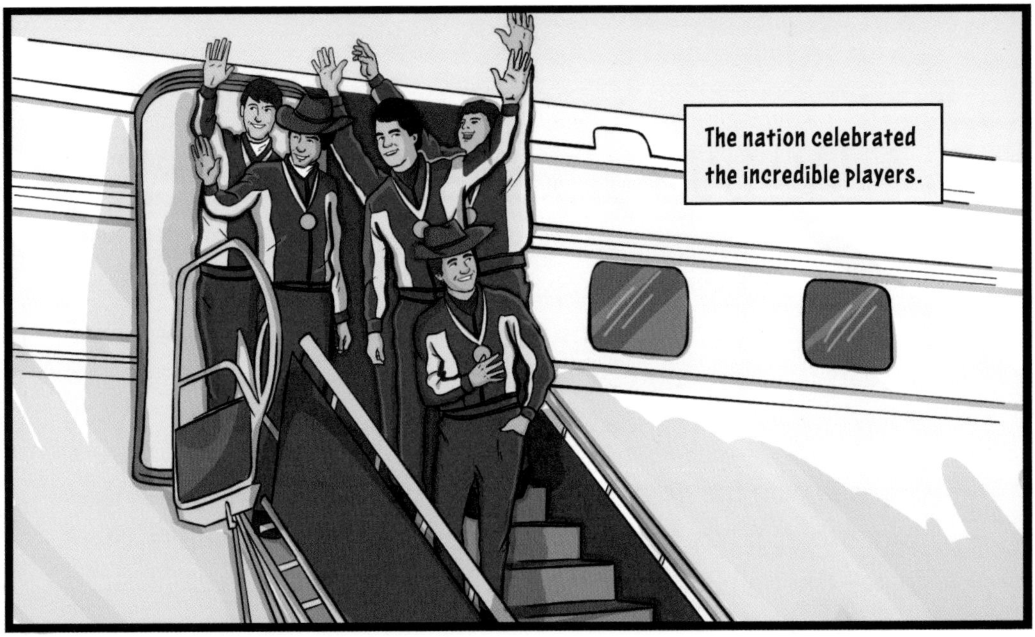
The nation celebrated the incredible players.

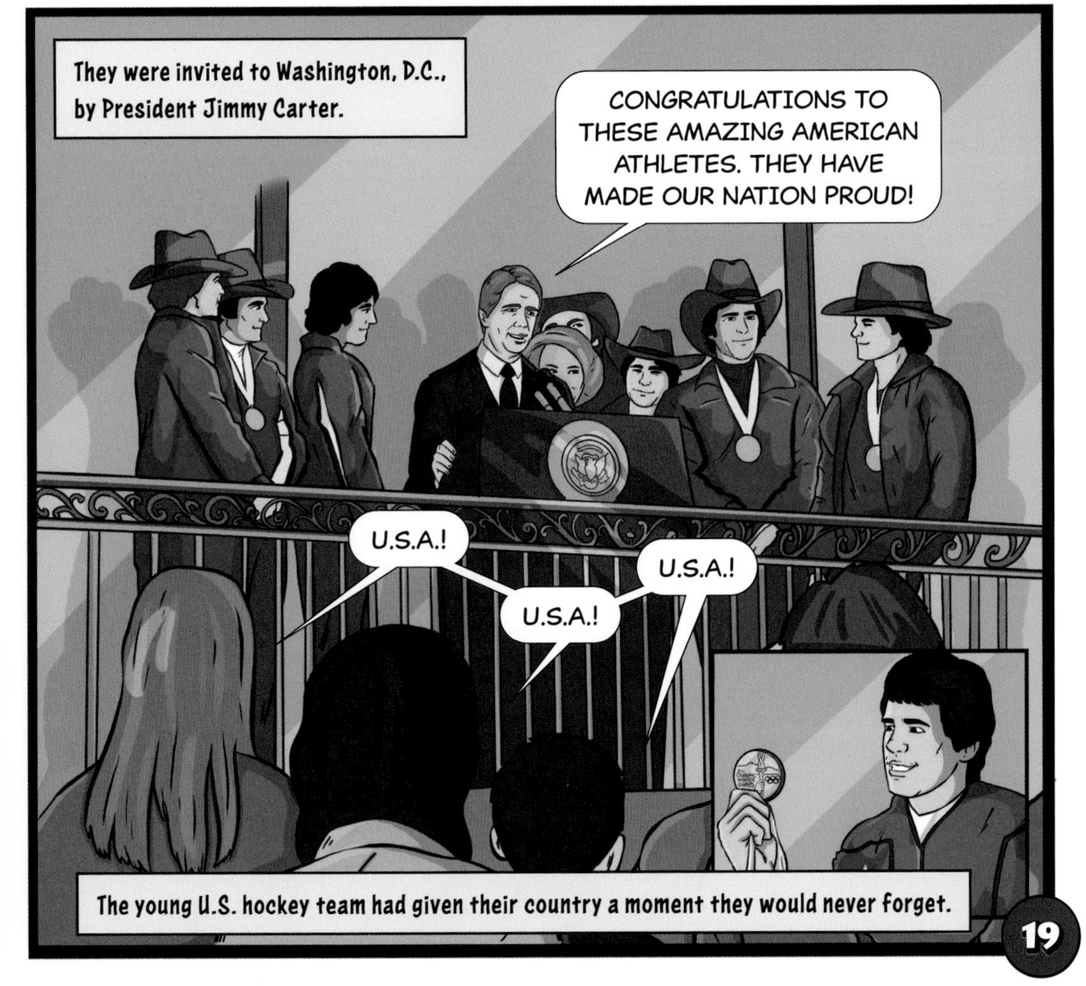
They were invited to Washington, D.C., by President Jimmy Carter.
CONGRATULATIONS TO THESE AMAZING AMERICAN ATHLETES. THEY HAVE MADE OUR NATION PROUD!
U.S.A.!
U.S.A.!
U.S.A.!
The young U.S. hockey team had given their country a moment they would never forget.

OLYMPIC HOCKEY HISTORY

The first Olympic ice hockey event was held during the 1920 Summer Olympics. Six nations played indoors in Antwerp, Belgium. Four years later, the sport switched to the Winter Olympics. Women's hockey was added to the Winter Games in 1992.

- Canada won the gold medal in the first Olympic hockey game. Since then, it has won the most men's gold medals—a total of nine—through 2022.

- The Soviet Union men's team won seven golds between 1956 and 1988.

- Including the 1980 win, the U.S. men have won gold twice. The first was in 1960.

- Only two countries have won gold medals in the women's competition. Canada has five of these medals and the United States has two.

- Three Canadian women hold the record for most Olympic hockey gold medals, with four each.

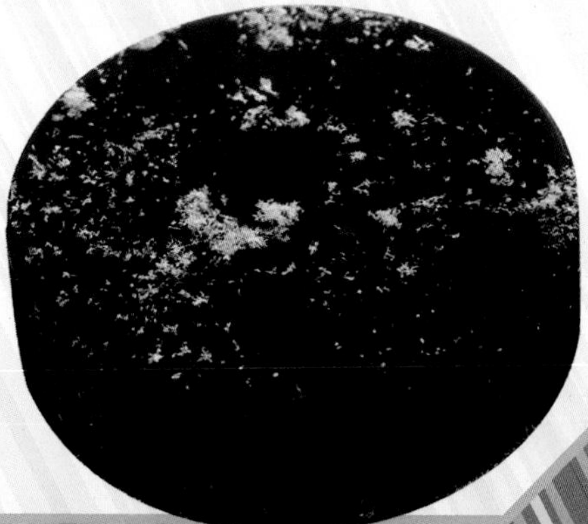

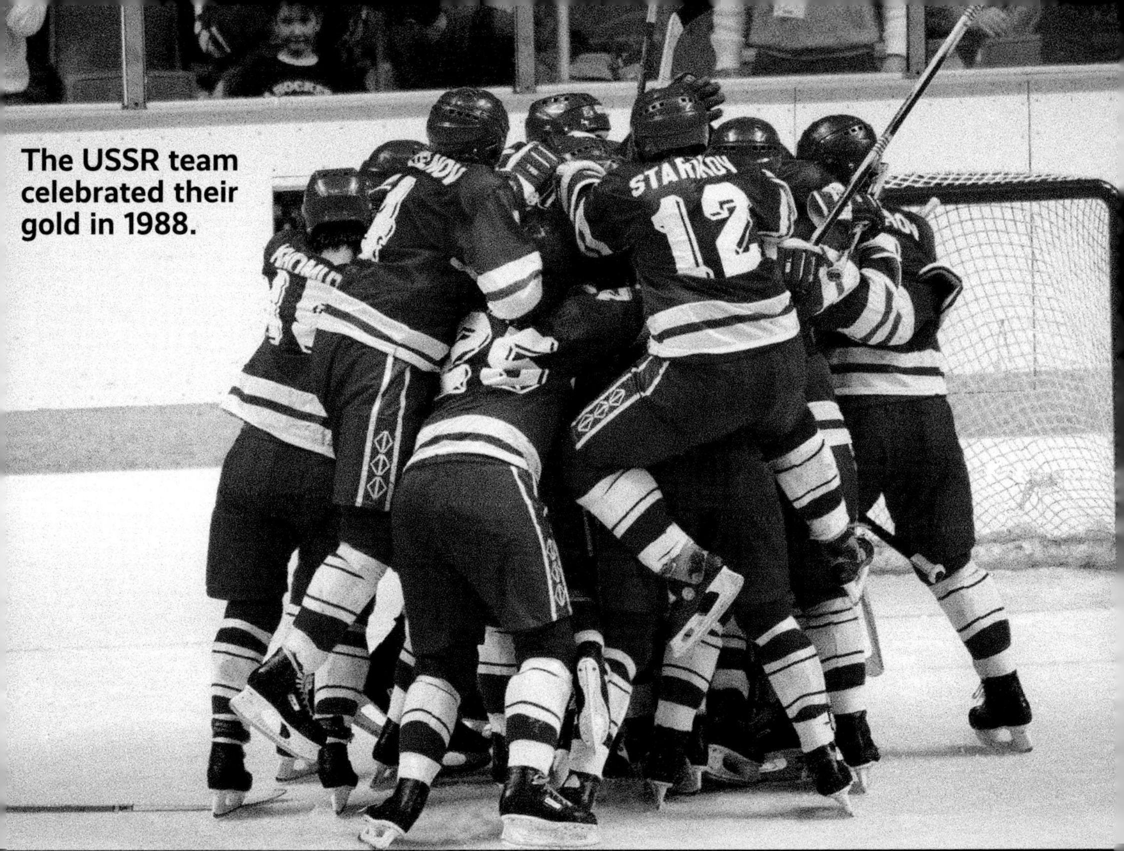
The USSR team celebrated their gold in 1988.

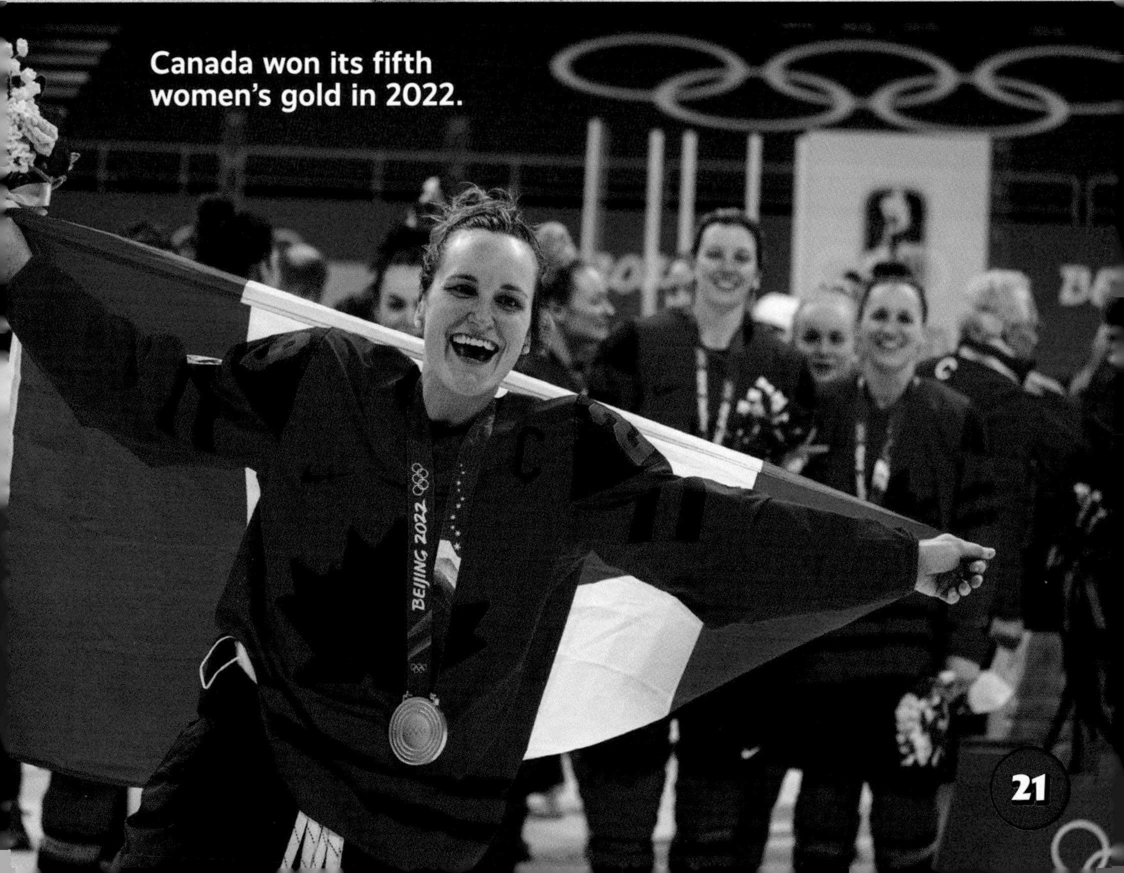
BEIJING 2022
Canada won its fifth women's gold in 2022.

OTHER OLYMPIC UPSETS

Magnificent Seven

From 1952 to 1992, women's gymnastics was dominated by the Soviet Union. The USSR won every team gold medal except one. But during the 1996 Summer Olympic Games in Atlanta, Georgia, the American women shocked the sports world. Led by Kerri Strug, they won the nation's first gymnastics team gold medal. Strug even performed her last vault with a badly sprained ankle!

Beating the Bear

Heading into the 2000 Olympics, Russian Alexandr Karelin was known as The Russian Bear—the most feared wrestler in the world. He had never lost a match, winning three gold medals in **Greco-Roman wrestling** in the process. But somehow, Rulon Gardner defeated him. The American earned just one point—the first that Karelin had given up in seven years—and won the match 1-0.

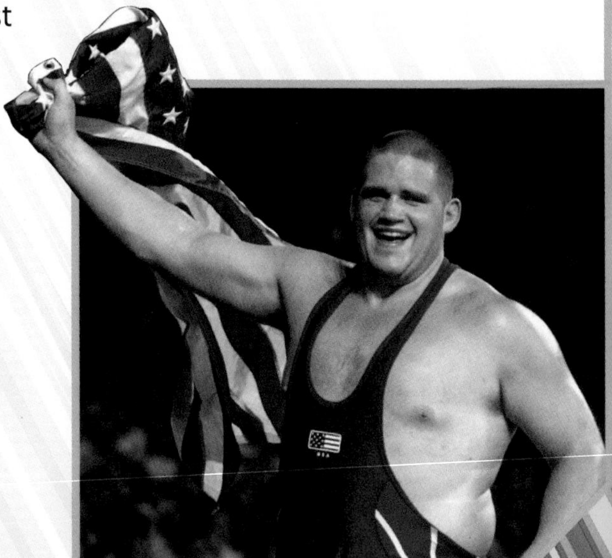

Rulon Gardner

GLOSSARY

Cold War a period of time from 1947 to 1991 in which the United States and other countries were in unofficial battle with the Soviet Union

dominated completely controlled and defeated

Greco-Roman wrestling a form of wrestling in which holds can be made only above the waist

invaded entered another country using military force with the goal of taking it over

nuclear weapons very powerful bombs that explode through the force of a nuclear reaction

period a 20-minute-long stretch of gameplay in hockey

power play when one team has more players on the ice after a player from the other team is sent out for a penalty

underdog a team or player that is not expected to win

upsets games that are won by a team that is not expected to win

23

INDEX

READ MORE

Doeden, Matt. *G.O.A.T. Hockey Teams (Greatest of All Time Teams).* Minneapolis: Lerner Publications, 2021.

Hoena, Blake. *Lake Placid Miracle: When U.S. Hockey Stunned the World (Graphic Library Greatest Sports Moments).* North Mankato, MN: Capstone Press, 2019.

Williams, Heather. *Miracle on Ice (Sports Unite Us).* Ann Arbor, MI: Cherry Lake, 2019.

LEARN MORE ONLINE

1. Go to **www.factsurfer.com** or scan the QR code below.
2. Enter **"Miracle on Ice"** into the search box.
3. Click on the cover of this book to see a list of websites.